WORLD'S FAVORITE SONGS

FOR

SINGING

AND

PLAYING

SELECTED AND ARRANGED BY

ALBERT GAMSE

FOREWORD

Many a volume in the "World's Favorite" series has been devoted to individual categories of songs, for instance, Songs of the Gay 90's, Folk Songs, Wedding Songs, Hootenanny Songs, etc.

This volume presents a group of songs that have been outstanding in just about every category or that do not fall within a specifically designated category. These are the really great songs of all time.

A unique feature of this collection is the dual utility of each song. Most of these songs have hitherto appeared with vocal line and non-melodic piano accompaniment. Here we present effective piano arrangements that lend themselves not only to the accompaniment of the singer but also to piano solo rendition. Chord names have been added to the melody lines of each selection.

This is an "all purpose" song book, because it caters to the concert singer, the balladeer, the family "sing along" gatherings, and it includes selections especially appropriate for various occasions.

We present it in full confidence that it will become a treasured addition to your music library.

The Publisher

© Copyright MCMLXIV by
ASHLEY PUBLICATIONS, INC.
263 Veterans Blvd., Carlstadt, N. J. 07072
International Copyright Secured   Made in U.S.A.

CONTENTS

CONTENTS

KASHMIRI SONG

(PALE HANDS I LOVED)

Words by
LAURENCE HOPE

Music by
AMY W. FINDEN

Moderato con sentimo

Pale hands I loved be-side the Sha-li-mar —, Where are you now? Who lies be-neath your spell?

FASCINATION

French lyric by
MAURICE deFERAUDY

English lyric by
ALBERT GAMSE

Music by
F. D. MARCHETTI

Valse moderato

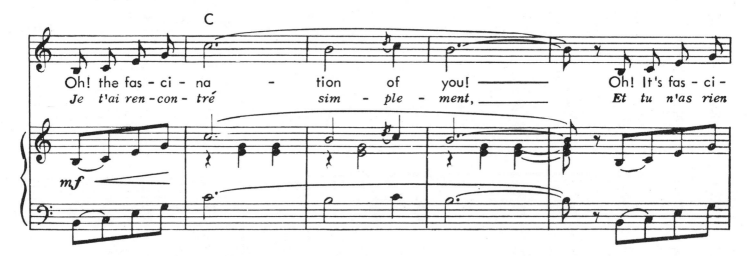

Oh! the fas - ci - na - tion of you! ____ Oh! It's fas - ci -
Je t'ai ren-con-tré sim - ple - ment,____ Et tu n'as rien

nat - ing to have you so near! ____ I re - mem - ber still ____
fait pour cher - cher à me plai - re,____ Je t'ai - me pour-tant

just fas-ci-nat-ed by you, Oh I love you, my dar-ling I do! _____
ché-ri, mon ai-mé, mon roi, Je n'ai de bon-heur qu'a-vec toi! _____

Be my own! Mine a-lone! Oh the fas-ci-na - tion of
Re-viens-moi Re-prends-moi Je t'ai ren-con-tré sim - ple -

you! _____ Oh it's fas-ci - nat-ing to have you so near! _____
ment, _____ Et tu n'as rien fait pour cher-cher à me plai - re, _____

_____ I re-mem-ber still _____ What a won-drous thrill _____ Came in-to my
_____ Je t'ai-me pour-tant _____ D'un a-mour ar - dent _____ Dont rien, je le

GYPSY LOVE SONG

Words by
HARRY B. SMITH

Music by
VICTOR HERBERT

TOYLAND

Words by
GLEN MacDONOUGH

Music by
VICTOR HERBERT

I'M CALLED LITTLE BUTTERCUP

Words by
W. S. GILBERT

Music by
ARTHUR SULLIVAN

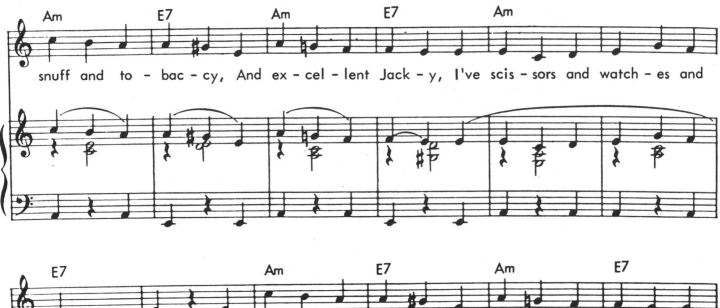

snuff and to - bac - cy, And ex - cel - lent Jack - y, I've scis - sors and watch - es and

knives, —————— I've rib - bons and lac - es to set off the fac - es — Of

pret - ty young sweet-hearts and wives. —————— I've trea - cle and tof - fee, I've

tea and I've cof - fee, Soft tom - my and suc - cu - lent chops, ————— I've

chick - ens and co - nies and pret - ty po - lo - nies, And ex - cel - lent pep-per-mint drops. ———————— Then buy of your But - ter - cup, Dear lit - tle But - ter - cup,

Sail - ors should nev - er be shy, ——————— So buy of your But - ter - cup,

Poor lit - tle But - ter - cup; Come! Of your But - ter - cup buy. ——————

TIT WILLOW

Words by
W. S. GILBERT

Music by
ARTHUR SULLIVAN

Andantino espressivo

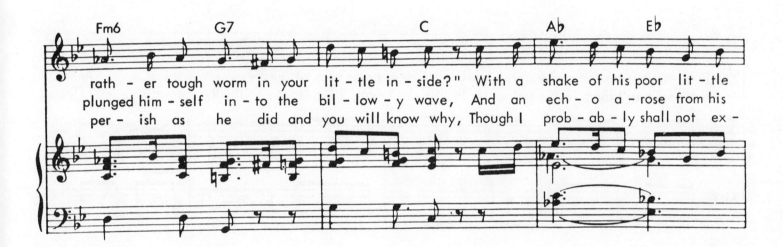

THE FLOWERS THAT BLOOM
IN THE SPRING

Words by
W. S. GILBERT

Music by
ARTHUR SULLIVAN

Allegro giocoso

that's what we mean when we say that a thing is wel-come as flow-ers that bloom in the spring, Tra
that's what I mean when I say or I sing "O both-er the flow-ers that bloom in the spring, Tra

la la la la —, tra la la la la —, The flow-ers that bloom in the spring. Tra
la la la la —, tra la la la la —, O both-er the flow-ers of spring. Tra

la la la la —, tra la la la la —, tra la la la la la.
la la la la —, tra la la la la —, tra la la la la la —————— la.

GOOD-BYE

Words by
WHYTE MELVILLE

Music by
F. PAOLO TOSTI

Andantino

Fall - ing leaf and fad - ing tree,

Lines of white in a sul - len sea, Shad - ows ris - ing on you and

Good — bye! ____

Hush! A voice from the far a-

way! "Lis-ten and learn," it seems — to say, "All the to-

mor-rows shall be as to-day", "All the to- mor-rows shall be as to-

day." The cord is frayed, the cruse is dry, The

link must break, and the lamp must — die. ——— Good-

bye to hope! Good-bye, Good-bye! Good-bye to

hope! Good-bye, Good —— bye! ———

What are we wait-ing for? Oh! my heart!

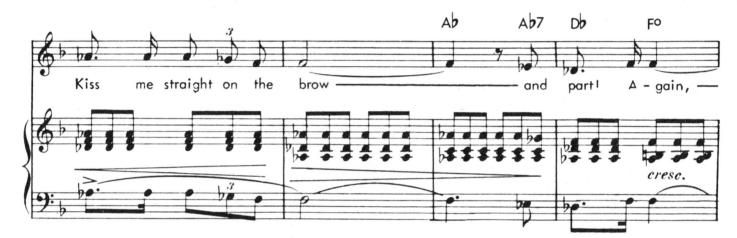

Kiss me straight on the brow ———————— and part! A-gain, ———

— a-gain! ——— My heart! My heart! What are we wait-ing

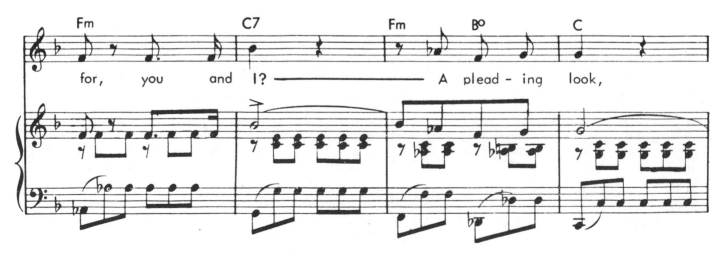

for, you and I? ——————————— A plead-ing look,

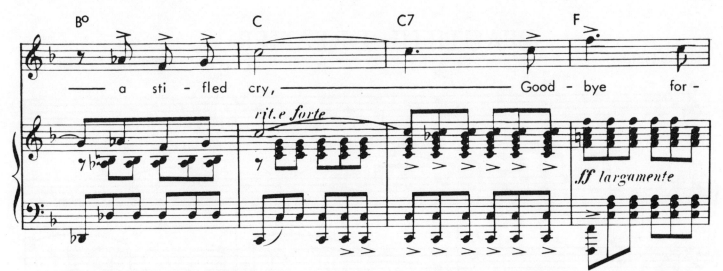

a sti-fled cry, — Good-bye for-

ev-er! Good-bye for-ev-er! Good-bye,

Good-bye, Good — bye! —

BEAUTIFUL DREAMER

Andantino

STEPHEN FOSTER

Beau-ti-ful dream - er, wake un - to me,

Star - light and dew - drops are wait - ing for thee,

Sounds of the rude world heard in the day,

Lull'd by the moon - light, have all passed a - way.

JEANIE WITH THE LIGHT BROWN HAIR

Moderato

STEPHEN FOSTER

I dream of Jean-ie with the

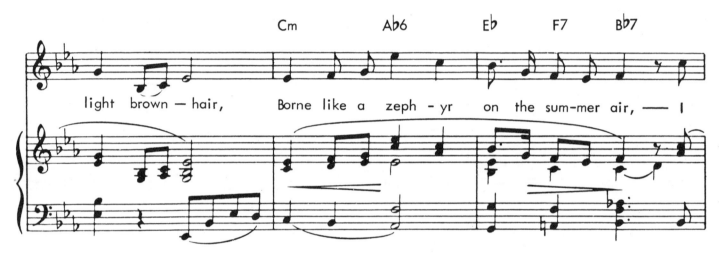

light brown — hair, Borne like a zeph-yr on the sum-mer air, — I

see her trip-ping where the bright streams — play,

Hap-py as the dais — ies that dance on her way.

Man - y were the wild notes her mer - ry voice would pour,

Man - y were the blithe birds that war - bled them o'er, Oh! I

dream of Jean - ie with the light brown — hair,

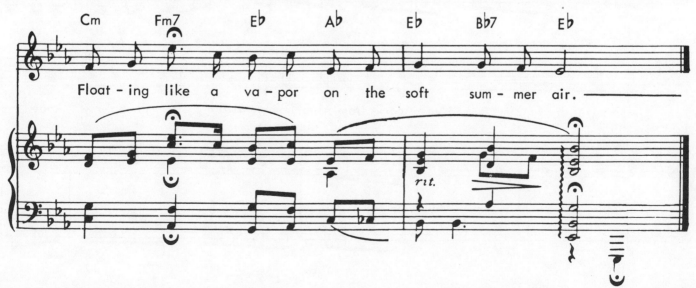

Float - ing like a va - por on the soft sum - mer air. —

OH! SUSANNA

Allegro vivace

STEPHEN FOSTER

CAMPTOWN RACES

STEPHEN FOSTER

OLD FOLKS AT HOME
(SWANEE RIVER)

STEPHEN FOSTER

1. Way down up-on the Swan-ee Riv-er,
2. All 'round the lit-tle farm I wan-der'd,
3. One lit-tle hut a-mong the bush-es,

Far, far a-way, There's where my heart am
When I was young, Then man-y hap-py
One that I love, Still sad-ly to my

turn-ing ev-er, There's where the old folks stay.
days I squan-der'd, Man-y the songs I sung.
mem-'ry rush-es —— No mat-ter where I rove.

THE OLD KENTUCKY HOME

Moderato

STEPHEN FOSTER

1. The sun shines bright on the old Ken-tuck-y home, ——— 'Tis
2. They hunt no more for the pos - sum and the coon, ——— On

sum-mer, the dark – ies are gay. ——————— The corn top's ripe and the
mead-ow, the hill and the shore. ——————— They sing no more by the

mead-ow is in bloom, While the birds make mu - sic all the
glim-mer of the moon, On the bench out - side the cab - in

CHORUS:

SOLVEJG'S SONG
(A SONG OF TRUE LOVE)

Andantino

EDUARD GRIEG

MY HEART AT THY SWEET VOICE

CAMILLE SAINT-SAENS

place my life, my all —— at thy beck and call. Thy voice, like won-drous

mu-sic, has a song I must hear, Speak to me, draw me near! ——

Molto più lento

Love! Oh let me hear —— the song of an —— gels high a-

bove me. —— Love! Oh let me hear —— the mag-ic

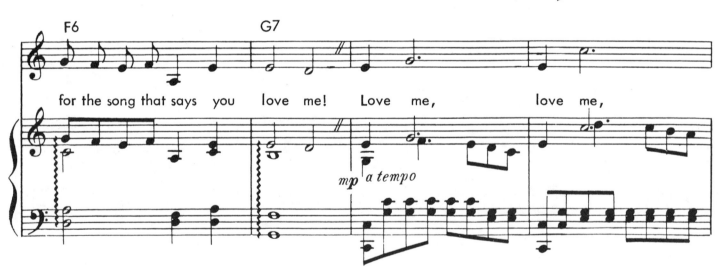

CRADLE SONG

JOHANNES BRAHMS

Andante (tenderly)

Lul — la — by and good
Gu - ten A - bend, gut'

night, With — ros — es be — dight —, Creep — in — to thy —
Nacht, mit Ro - sen be - dacht,___ mit Näg - lein be -

bed, There — pil — low thy head. If God will, thou shalt
steckt schulpf' un - ter die Deck: Mor - gen früh wenn Got

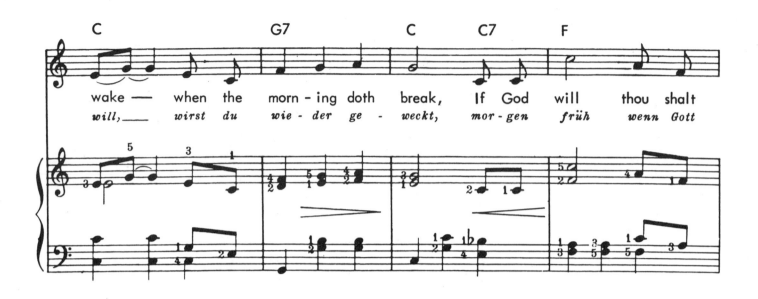

wake — when the morn - ing doth break, If God will thou shalt
will,___ wirst du wie - der ge - weckt, mor - gen früh wenn Gott

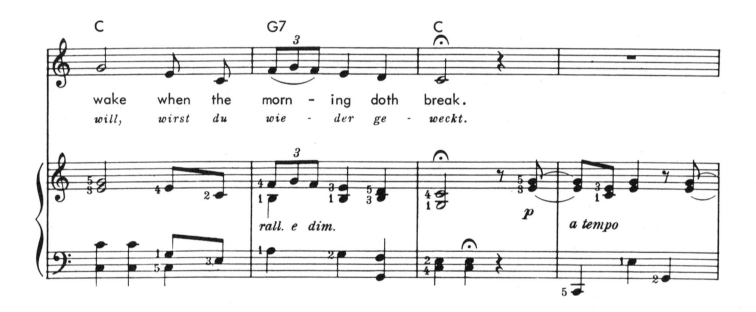

wake when the morn - ing doth break.
will, wirst du wie - der ge - weckt.

rall. e dim.   p   a tempo

Lul - la - by and good night, Those — blue eyes close tight —, Bright —
Gu - ten A - bend, gut' Nacht, von Eng'- lein be - wackt, die

p

an - gels are — near, So — sleep — with-out fear. They will
zei - gen im Traum dir Christ - kind - leins Baum: Schlaf' nun

guard thee from harm, With fair dream - land's sweet charm, They will
se - lig und süss, Schau' im Traum's Pa - ra - dies, schlaf' nun

guard thee from harm, With fair dream - land's sweet charm.
se - lig und süss schau' im Traum's Pa - ra - dies.

rall. e dim.

NONE BUT THE LONELY HEART

Poem by
JOH. GOETHE

Music by
PETER ILYICH TSCHAIKOWSKY

Andante

None but the lone — ly heart —
Nur wer die Sehn ___ sucht kennt,

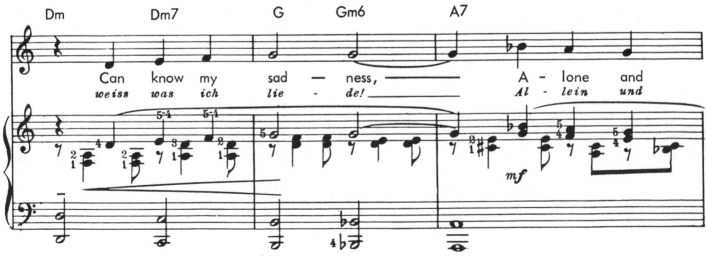

Can know my sad — ness, ——— A - lone and
weiss was ich lie - de! ——— Al - lein und

SERENADE

FRANZ SCHUBERT

Moderato con moto

Lis-ten my love, oh lis-ten my love, I send my heart in a song,
Lei-se fle-hen mei-ne Lie-der durch die Nacht zu dir,

Here to thy cham-ber window my dar-ling, Love has brought me a-long.
in den stil-len Hain hernie-der, Lieb-chen,komm zu mir:

While the stars a-bove are gleam-ing, Mu-sic is soft-ly
Flüsternd schlan-ke Wipfel-rau-schen in des Mon-des

played,   Mu-sic is soft - ly   played.   As of you   my heart keeps dream-ing,
Licht,   in des Mon - des Licht,   des Ver-rä - thers feindlich Lau - schen

This is my se - re - nade,   This is my se - re - nade!
fürchte, Hol - de, nicht   fürchte, Hol - de, nicht.

Lis-ten my love,   oh lis-ten my love, The winds are echoing me!
Hörst die Nach - ti - gallen schlagen? ack! sie flehen dich,

Won't you try to see? ——————— You're the one—my heart is need-ing,
Lieb - chen, höre mich, *be - bend harr' ich dir entge - gen,*

Dar-ling oh come to me!   Dar-ling oh come to me!
komm, beglü - cke mich!   *komm, beglü - cke mich* _____

Dar-ling, come   to   me!
be - glü - cke   mich!

ESTRELLITA
(LITTLE STAR)

English words by
ALBERT GAMSE

Music and
Spanish words by
MANUEL PONCE

Andante moderato

Es-trel-li - ta, lit-tle star, keep gleam-ing, Send
Es-tre-lli - ta del le-ja - no cie-lo Que

down your love-ly light - To cheer my lone-ly night, Es-trel-li - ta, lit-tle star, while
mi-ras mi do-lor, que sa-bes mi su-frir, ba-ja y di - me si me quie-re un

beam - ing, Do not hide be - hind a cloud to-night, Keep shin-ing bright till
po - co Por-que yo no pue - do sin su a - mor vi -

morn. _____ Es - trel - li - ta, lit-tle star, I'm dream-ing, That
vir. _____ Es - tre - lli - ta del le - ja - no cie - lo, Que

on a dis - tant shore, I'll find my love once more, So I'm
mi - ras mi do - lor, que sa - bes mi su - frir. ba - ja y

plead - ing, lit - tle star, keep gleam - ing, Do not take a - way your
di - me si me quie re un po - co. Por-que yo no

Eb · · Bb° · Bb7 · Eb · Bb7

friend-ly glow and leave me so for-lorn. — You heard our good-bye from your
pue - do sin su a-mor vi - vir. _____ Tu e - res es-tre - lla mi

Eb · Fm7 · Bb7 · Abm · Eb

heav-en-ly throne, and now you and I share the night a-lone, Es - trel -
fa - ro de a-mor. Tu sa-bes que pron - to he de mo-rir. Ba - ja y

Eb+ · Ab6 · Eb°

li - ta, lit-tle star, I'm schem - ing, With the guid-ance of your
di - me si me quie - re un po - co, Por-que yo no

Eb · Bb° · Bb7 · Eb

silv - 'ry ray, a new love may be born.
pue - do sin su a - mor vi - vir.

L.H.

COME BACK TO SORRENTO

ERNESTO de CURTIS

1. Oh how deep is my de - vo - tion,
2. I keep dream-ing of Sor - ren - to,

1. *Guar-da il ma - re co m'è, bel - lo!*
2. *Ve di il ma - re di Sor - ren - to,*

Oh how sweet is my e - mo - tion,   As in dreams I cross an o - cean —
For I met you in Sor - ren - to,   And you gave me a me - men - to —

spi-ra tan-to sen-ti - men - to,   co-me il tuo soa-ve ac - cen - to
che te-so-ri ce la in fon-do: chi ha gi-ra - to tut-to il mon - do

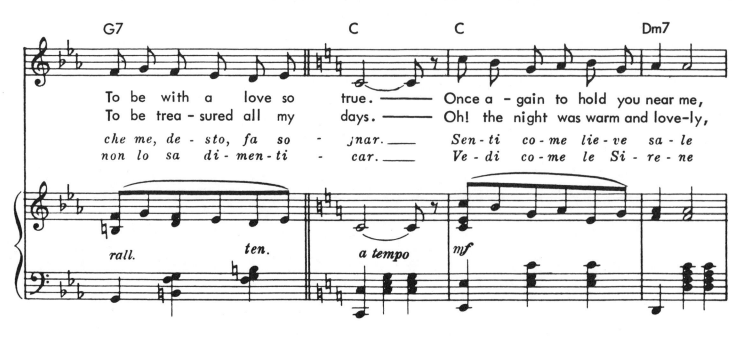

To be with a love so true.——— Once a-gain to hold you near me,
To be trea-sured all my days.——— Oh! the night was warm and love-ly,
che me, de - sto, fa so - jnar.___ Sen - ti co - me lie - ve sa - le
non lo sa di - men - ti - car.___ Ve - di co - me le Si - re - ne

Once a-gain to kiss you dear-ly, Once a-gain to let you hear me———
Stars were in the sky a - bove me, And your kiss de - clared you love me———
dai giar - di - ni o - dor d'a - ran - ci: un pro - fu - mo non v'hue - gua - le
or ti guar - dano in - can - ta - te, par che vo - glia - no a te so - la

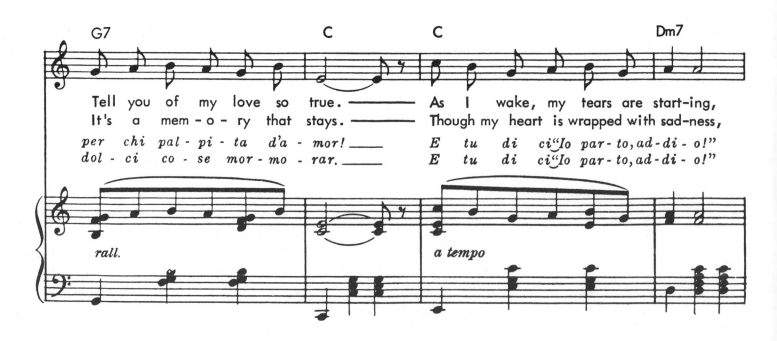

Tell you of my love so true.——— As I wake, my tears are start-ing,
It's a mem-o-ry that stays.——— Though my heart is wrapped with sad-ness,
per chi pal - pi - ta d'a - mor!___ E tu di ci "Io par - to, ad - di - o!"
dol - ci co - se mor - mo - rar.___ E tu di ci "Io par - to, ad - di - o!"

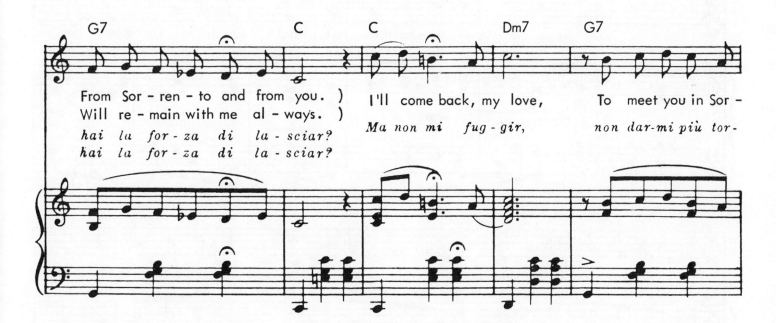

O SOLE MIO

EDUARDO di CAPUA

Andante moderato

Be - hold the bril - liant sun in all its splen - dor,
Che bel - la co - sa 'na iur-na-ta'e so - le,

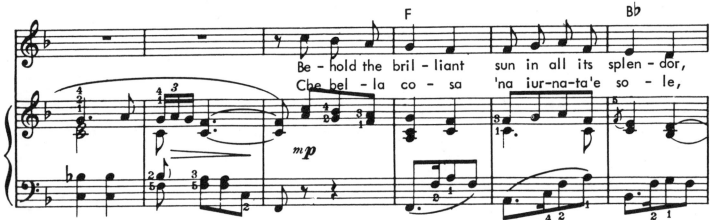

For-got-ten is the storm, The clouds now van - ish,
N'a-ria se - re - na dop — po 'na tem-pes — ta!
The fresh'ning breez-es pe' ll'a - ria fres - ca

heav-y airs will ban - ish, Be-hold the bril - liant sun in all its splen-dor!
pa - re già 'na fe - sta, — Che bel - la co - sa 'na iur - na - ta'e so — le.

Refrain

A sun I know of —— that's bright-er still, —— That sun, my
Ma n'a-tu so — le —— cchiù bel-lo, ohi - ne', —— 'o so - le

dear - est, —— is naught but thee, —— Thy face ——
mi - o —— sta - nfron - te a te! —— 'O so ——

—— so fair to see, That —— shall now my sun —— for - ev - er be!
—— le 'o so - le mi - o —— sta - nfron - te 'a te, —— sta - nfron - te a te!

2.

Lùcene 'e llastre d' 'a fenesta toia;
'na lavannara canta e se ne vanta,
e pe' tramente torce, spanne e canta,
lùcene 'e llastre d' 'a fenesta toia.
 Ma n'atu sole
 cchiù bello, ohi ne',
 'o sole mio
 sta nfronte a te!

3.

Quanno fa notte e 'o sole se ne scenne,
mme vene quase 'na malincunia,
sotto 'a fenesta toia restarria,
quanno fa notte e 'o sole se ne scenne;
 Ma n'atu sole
 cchiù bello, ohi ne',
 'o sole mio
 sta nfronte a te!

ELEGIE

JULES MASSENET

SPRING SONG

FELIX MENDELSSOHN

Spring! With-in my heart I sing a song of Spring, A song of rob-ins

in the trees and flow-ers bright-ly gleam-ing, Oh come and share the

beau-ty of these days with me, Oh can't you see — I need you to be

near to me, for you're my ev-'ry-thing, I need you to be near to me to

IN OLD MADRID

Words by
CLIFTON BINGHAM

Music by
H. TROTÉRE

Bolero moderato

1. Long years a -
2. Far, far a -

go,   In old Ma - drid,   Where soft-ly sighs of love the light gui-tar,   Two spark-ling
way   from old Ma - drid,   Her lov-er fell long years a - go for Spain.   A con - vent

eyes - a lat-tice hid,   Two eyes as dark-ly bright as love's own star!   There
veil those sweet eyes hid,   And all the vows that love had sighed were vain.   But

on the case-ment ledge when day was o'er,   A   ti - ny hand   was
still be - tween the dusk and night, 'tis said,   Her   white hand opes   the

BARCAROLLE
(LOVELY NIGHT)

JACQUES OFFENBACH

Allegretto moderato

Love - ly night, oh night — of love, oh beau - ti - ful night of bliss, ——

Long have I been dream — ing of a beau - ti - ful night like this. ——

Here we are where ev-'ry star can see the kiss we share,

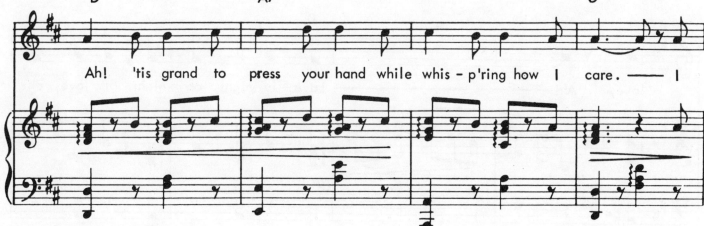

Ah! 'tis grand to press your hand while whis-p'ring how I care. —— I

pledge my love to you —————— un-der heav-ens of blue, —— I

pledge my love so true, Say that you love me too! This is a

night made for love, This is a night made for

love, Ah! ———————————— Love - ly night, oh night of love, oh

beau-ti-ful night of bliss, Long have I been dream-ing of a

beau-ti-ful night like this. ——— Oh I love you, I do!

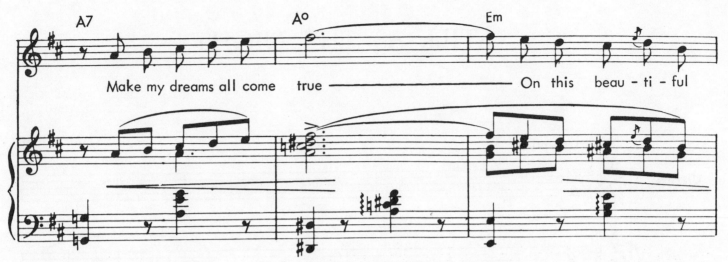

Make my dreams all come true —————————— On this beau - ti - ful

night, this love ———ly night! Ah! ——— Ah! ———

Ah! ——— Ah! ——— Ah! ——— Ah! ———

STILL AS THE NIGHT

CARL BOHM

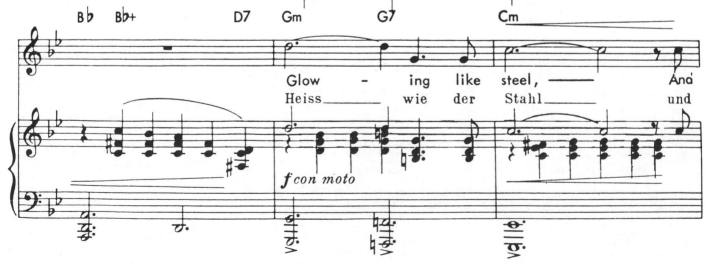

HARK! HARK! THE LARK

FRANZ SCHUBERT

Allegretto

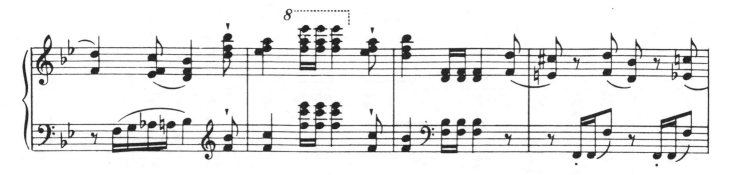

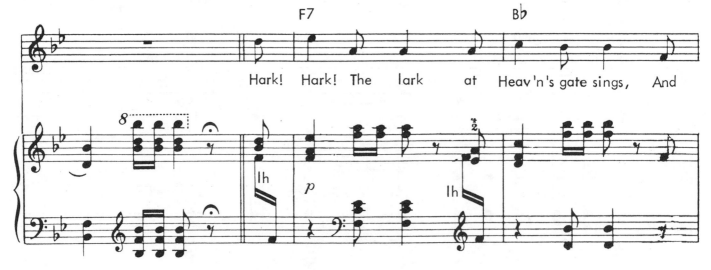

Hark! Hark! The lark at Heav'n's gate sings, And

Phoe —bus 'gins — to rise, ———— His steeds to wa - ter at those springs, On

MIGHTY LAK'A ROSE

Words by
FRANK L. STANTON

Music by
ETHELBERT NEVIN

A DREAM

Words by
J. C. BARTLETT

Music by
CHARLES B. CORY

night I was dream-ing, Of thee, love, was dream-ing, I dream'd thou didst prom-ise we nev-er-should part. While thy lov'd voice ad-dressed me,—And

THE ROSARY

Words by
ROBERT C. ROGERS

Music by
ETHELBERT NEVIN

Each hour a pearl, each pearl a pray'r — To still a heart in ab - sence
U - ne pri - ère à cha - que grain Pour cal - mer mon coeur aux a -
Wie sie, so reiht der Stun - den Zahl, Ein lich - ter Kranz, sich je - des -

wrung, I tell each bead un - to the end, And there a
bois, J'ar - rive ain - si jus - qu'à la fin, Mais là pend
mal Zur Ket - te von Ge - be - ten fromm-- Bis ich zum

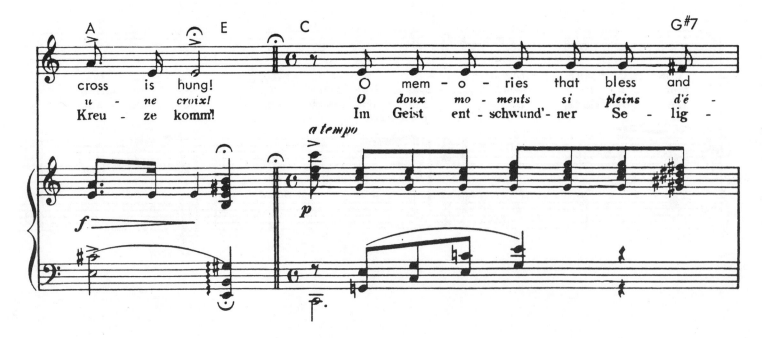

cross is hung! O mem - o - ries that bless and
u - ne croix! O doux mo - ments si pleins d'é -
Kreu - ze komm! Im Geist ent - schwund'- ner Se - lig -

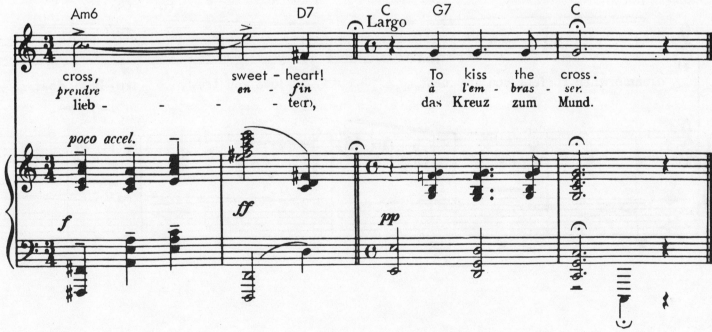

I LOVE YOU TRULY

CARRIE JACOBS-BOND

HOW CAN I LEAVE THEE?

TRADITIONAL

Moderato

| Bb | Eb | Bb | F7 | Eb | F7 | Bb | Eb | Bb | C#o | Bb |

1. Ach, wie ist's mög-lich dann, dass ich dich las-sen kann! hab' dich von
2. Blau ist ein Blü-me-lein, das heisst Ver-giss-nicht-mein; dies Blüm-lein
3. Wär' ich ein Vö-ge-lein, wollt' ich bald bei dir sein, scheut' Falk und

How can I leave — thee! From thee how can I part? Thou on-ly

| Eb | Bb | C7 | F | F7 | Bb | Eb | Bb | G7 |

Her-zen lieb, das glau-be mir! Du hast das Her-ze mein so ganz ge-
leg' an's Herz, und denk' an mich! Stirbt Blum' und Hoff-nung gleich, wir sind an
Ha-bicht nicht, flög' schnell zu dir. Schöss mich ein Jä-ger todt, fiel' ich in

hast my heart, My love, my own! Thou hast this soul of mine, So close-ly

| Cm | G7 | Cm | F7 | Bb | Eb | Bb | C7 | F7 | Bb |

nom-men ein, dass ich kein' An-dre lieb', als dich al-lein.
Lie-be reich; denn die stirbt nie bei mir; das glau-be mir!
dei-nen Schoss; säh'st du mich trau-rig an, gern stürb' ich dann!

bound to thine, No oth-er can I love, Save thee a-lone!

THE LAST ROSE OF SUMMER

FRIEDRICH von FLOTOW

IN THE GLOAMING

Words by
META ORRED

Music by
ANNIE HARRISON

In the gloam - ing, Oh my dar - ling! When the lights are dim and
In the gloam - ing, Oh my dar - ling! Think not bit - ter - ly of

low, And the qui - et shad - ows fall - ing, Soft - ly come and
me! Though I passed a - way in si - lence, Left you lone - ly -

soft - ly go, When the winds are sob - bing faint - ly, With a
set you free, For my heart was crushed with long - ing, What had

AURA LEE

TRADITIONAL

Moderato

mf

mp

Bb   Cm   C7   F7   Bb

1. As the black-bird in the spring, — 'Neath the wil - low tree ———,
3. In her blush the rose was born, 'Twas mu - sic when she spake ———,

Bb   Cm   C7   F7   Bb

Sat and piped, I heard him sing, In praise of Au - ra Lee. ———
In her eyes, the light of morn, — Spark-ling, seemed to break. ———

Bb   D7   Gm   Cm6   D

Au - ra Lee, Au - ra Lee, Maid with gold - en hair, ———
Au - ra Lee, Au - ra Lee, Maid with gold - en hair, ———

f

Sun - shine came a - long with thee, And swal-lows in the air. 2. Take my heart and
Sun - shine came a - long with thee, And swal-lows in the air. 4. Au - ra Lee, the

take my ring, I give my all to thee ——, Take me for e - ter - ni - ty,
bird may flee, The wil - low's gold-en hair ——, Swing thro' win-ter fit - full - y,

Dear-est Au - ra Lee! — Au - ra Lee, Au - ra Lee, Maid with gold - en hair,
On the storm - y air. — Yet if thy blue eyes I see, Gloom will soon de - part,

Sun-shine came a - long with thee, And swal-lows in the air. ——
For to me, sweet Au - ra Lee, Is sun - shine to the heart. ——

MY BONNIE

TRADITIONAL

Valse moderato

1. My Bon-nie lies o-ver the o-cean. ———— My Bon-nie lies o-ver the
2. Last night as I lay on my pil-low. ———— Last night as I lay on my

sea. ———— My Bon-nie lies o-ver the o-cean. ———— Oh bring back my
bed, ———— Last night as I lay on my pil-low, ———— I dreamt that my

Bon-nie to me.) ———— Bring back, bring back, Bring back my Bon-nie to
Bon-nie was dead.)

me, to me. ——— Bring back, bring back, Oh bring back my Bon-nie to me. ———

CARRY ME BACK TO OLD VIRGINNY

JAMES BLAND

Moderato

Car - ry me back to old Vir - gin - ny,

There's where the cot-ton and the corn and 'ta-toes grow. — There's where the birds war-ble

sweet in the spring-time, There's where the old dar-key's heart am long to go. —

Fine

There's where I la - bored so hard for old mas - sa, Day af - ter day in the

field of yel - low corn. —— No place on earth do I love more sin-cere-ly —

Than old Vir - gin-ny, The— State where I was born. Car-ry me back to

Old Vir - gin-ny, There let me live till I with - er and de-cay. ——

AFTER THE BALL

CHARLES K. HARRIS

Valse moderato

After the ball is o - ver, Af - ter the break of morn, —

Af - ter the danc — ers leav - ing, Af - ter the stars are gone, —

Man - y a heart is ach - ing, If you could read them all, —

Man - y the hopes that have van - ished, Af - ter the ball. — ball. —

IN THE GOOD OLD SUMMERTIME

Words by
REN SHIELDS

Music by
GEORGE EVANS

In the good old sum-mer time, ——— In the good old sum-mer time ———

Stroll-ing thro' the sha-dy lanes, With your "ba-by mine", ——— You

hold her hand and she holds yours, And that's a ve-ry good sign, — That she's your

toot-sey woot-sey in the good old sum-mer time. ——— In the time. ———

KENTUCKY BABE

Music by
ADAM GEIBEL

Words by
RICHARD BUCK

Moderato

'Skeet - ers am a hum - min' on the hon-ey suck - le vine,   Sleep, Ken-tuck-y

Babe! —————————— Sand-man am a - com - in' to this lit - tle babe of mine, ——

MY GAL SAL

PAUL DRESSER

Ev - 'ry-thing is o - ver and I'm feel - ing bad, —
Brought her lit - tle dain - ties just a - fore she died, —

I lost the best pal that I ev - er had. 'Tis but a fort - night
Prom-ised she would meet me on the oth - er side. Told her how I loved her,

since she was here. — Seems like she's gone though for twen - ty year —
she said "I know, Jim" — Just do your best, leave the rest to Him. —

THE ROSE OF TRALEE

Words by
C. M. SPENCER

Music by
C. W. GLOVER

Andante (tenderly)

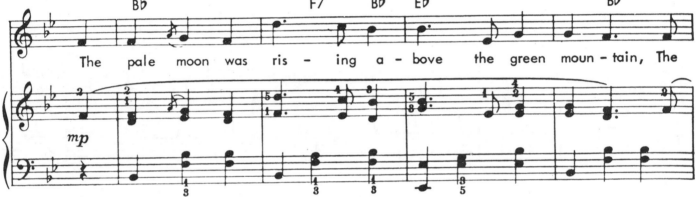

The pale moon was ris - ing a - bove the green moun - tain, The

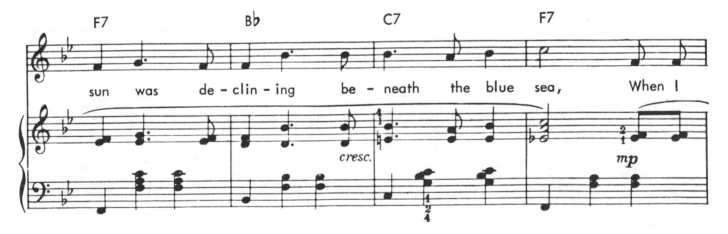

sun was de - clin - ing be - neath the blue sea, When I

strayed with my love to the pure crys - tal foun - tain, That

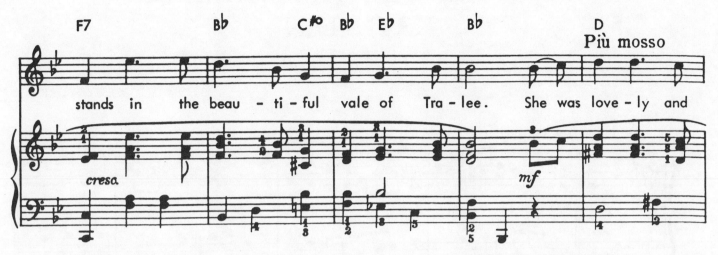

I'LL TAKE YOU HOME AGAIN, KATHLEEN

THOMAS P. WESTENDORF

Andante con espressione

1. I'll take you home a-gain, Kath-leen, A-cross the o-cean wild and wide, —— To
2. I know you love me Kath-leen, dear, Your heart was ev-er fond and true, —— I
3. To that dear home be-yond the sea, My Kath-leen shall a-gain re-turn, —— And

where your heart has ev-er been, Since first you were my bon-ny bride. The
al-ways feel when you are near, That life holds noth-ing dear but you, The
when thy old friends wel-come thee, Thy lov-ing heart will cease to yearn, Where

SILVER THREADS AMONG THE GOLD

Words by
EBEN E. REXFORD

Music by
HART P. DANKS

Andante moderato

1. Dar - ling, I am grow - ing old, _____ Sil - ver threads a - mong the
2. When your hair is sil - ver white, _____ And your cheeks no long - er
3. Love can nev - er more grow old, _____ Locks may lose their brown and
4. Love is al - ways young and fair, _____ What to us is sil - ver

gold, _____ Shine up - on my brow to - day, _____
bright, _____ With the ros - es of the May, _____
gold, _____ Cheeks may fade and hol - low grow, _____
hair, _____ Fad - ed cheeks or steps grown slow, _____

Life is fad - ing fast a - way, ——— But, my dar - ling, you will
I will kiss your lips and say ——— Oh, my dar - ling, mine a-
But the hearts that love will know ——— Nev - er, nev - er win - ter's
To the hearts that beat be - low? ——— Since I kissed you, mine a-

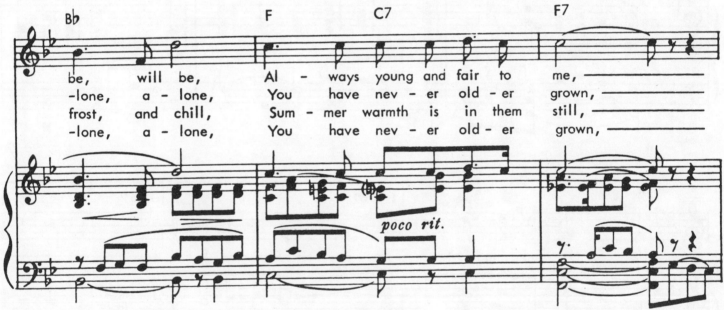

be, will be, Al - ways young and fair to me, ———
-lone, a - lone, You have nev - er old - er grown, ———
frost, and chill, Sum - mer warmth is in them still, ———
-lone, a - lone, You have nev - er old - er grown, ———

Yes, my dar - ling, you will be, ——— Al - ways young and fair to me. ———
Yes, my dar - ling, mine a - lone, ——— You have nev - er old - er grown. ———
Nev - er win - ter's frost and chill, ——— Sum - mer warmth is in them still. ———
Since I kissed you, mine a - lone, ——— You have nev - er old - er grown. ———

CHORUS

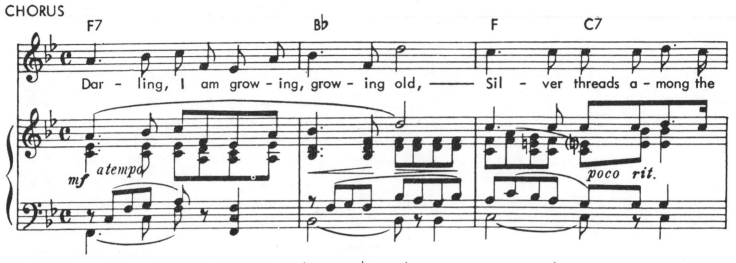

Dar - ling, I am grow - ing, grow - ing old, —— Sil - ver threads a - mong the

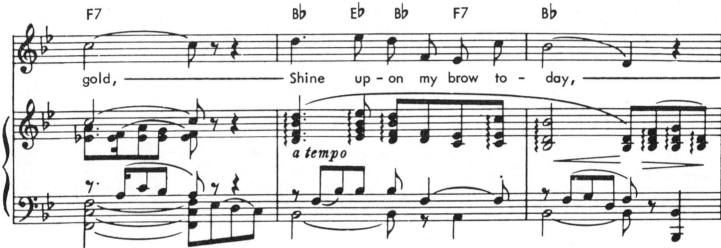

gold, ———————— Shine up - on my brow to - day, ——

Life is fad - ing fast a - way. ————— way. ——

Play after last Chorus

THE SIDEWALKS OF NEW YORK
(EAST SIDE, WEST SIDE)

Words by
CHARLES B. LAWLOR

Music by
JAMES W. BLAKE

THE SWEETEST STORY EVER TOLD

R. M. STULTS

Andante con espressione

Tell me, do you love me? Tell me soft-ly, sweet-ly, as of old!

Tell me that you love me, For that's the sweet-est sto-ry ev-er told.

Tell me, do you love me? Whis-per soft-ly, sweet-ly as of old. ———

Tell me that you love me, For that's the sweet — est sto-ry ev — er

told.

THE YELLOW ROSE OF TEXAS

TRADITIONAL

With spirit
Marcato

Verses

There's a yel-low rose in Tex-as I'm goi-ing there to see. — No oth-er fel-low
(Oh, I'm) go - ing back to find her, my heart is full of woe. — We'll sing the songs to-

knows her, No - bod - y, on - ly me. — She cried so, when I left her, It
geth - er, that we sang so long a - go. — I'll pick the ban-jo gai - ly, and

like to broke her heart, And if we ev-er meet a-gain, we nev - er more shall part.
sing the songs of yore, The Yel-low Rose of Tex-as, she'll be mine for-ev - er - more.

CHORUS

She's the sweet-est rose of col-or a fel-low ev-er knew, Her eyes are bright as dia-monds, They spark-le like the dew. You may talk a-bout your dear-est maids and sing of Ro-sy Lee, But The Yel-low Rose of Tex-as beats the belles of Ten-nes-see. Oh, I'm belles of Ten-nes- see.

DEAR OLD GIRL

Words by
RICHARD BUCK

Music by
THEODORE MORSE

Andante moderato

Dear Old Girl, the rob-in sings a-bove you, Dear Old Girl, it speaks of how I love you. The blind-ing tears are falling, As I think of my lost pearl, And my brok-en heart is call-ing, Call-ing for you, Dear Old Girl. Dear Old for you, Dear Old Girl.

MY WILD IRISH ROSE

CHAUNCEY OLCOTT

If you lis - ten, I'll sing you a sweet lit - tle
They may sing of their ros - es which by oth - er

song — Of a flow - er that's now drooped and dead. —— Yet dear - er to
names, Would smell just as sweet - ly, they say, —— But I know that my

me, Yes, than all of its mates, Tho' each holds a - loft its proud head. ——'Twas
Rose —— would nev - er con - sent - To have that sweet name tak - en a - way. —— Her

GIVE MY REGARDS TO BROADWAY

Marcato moderato

GEORGE M. COHAN

GIVE MY RE - GARDS TO BROAD - WAY, Re -

mem - ber me to Her - ald Square.

Tell all the gang at For - ty Sec - ond Street that

I will soon be there.

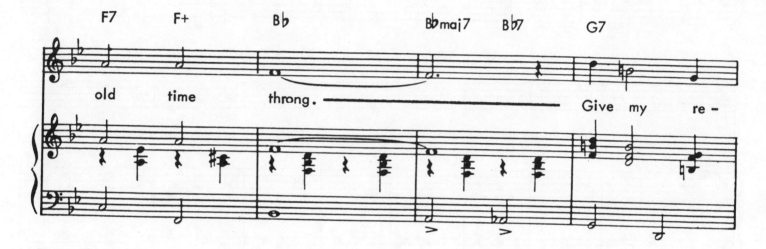

SWEET ROSIE O'GRADY

MAUD NUGENT

HOME ON THE RANGE

Western Song

Valse andantino

1. Oh give me a
2. Oh give me a
3. Where the air is so
4. How of – ten at

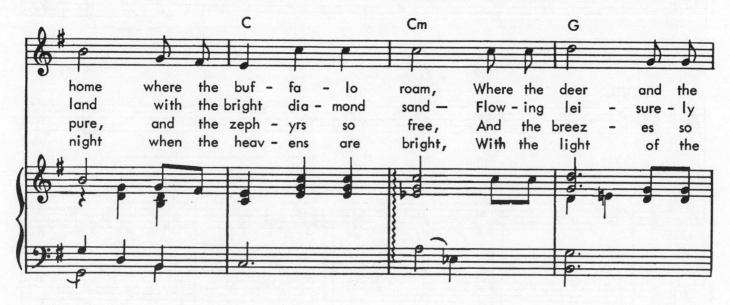

home where the buf – fa – lo roam, Where the deer and the
land with the bright dia – mond sand – Flow – ing lei – sure – ly
pure, and the zeph – yrs so free, And the breez – es so
night when the heav – ens are bright, With the light of the

an - te - lope play, ———— Where sel - dom is heard a dis-
down the clear stream, ———— Where the grace - ful white swan goes —
balm - y and bright, ———— That I would not ex - change my —
glit - ter - ing stars, ———— Have I stood there a - mazed and —

cour - ag - ing word, And the skies are not cloud - y all day. ————
glid - ing a - long, Like a maid in a heav - en - ly dream. ————
home on the range — For — all of the cit - ies so bright. ————
asked as I gazed — If their glo - ry ex - ceeds that of ours. ————

CHORUS

Home, Home on the range, ———————————— Where the

deer and the an-te-lope play, ——————— Where

sel-dom is heard a dis-cour-ag-ing word — And the

skies are not cloud-y all day. ——————— D.S.

D.S.

day. ——————

HOME SWEET HOME

Words by
JOHN H. PAYNE

Music by
HENRY R. BISHOP

Andantino

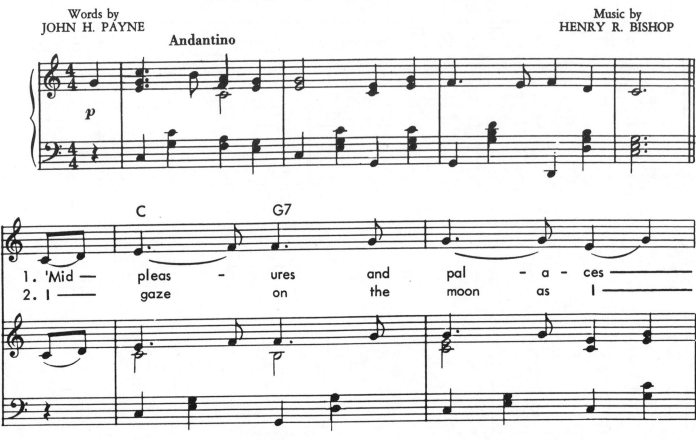

1. 'Mid — pleas - ures and pal - a - ces — though — we may roam, Be it ev — er so
2. I — gaze on and the moon as I — tread — the drear wild, And — feel — that my

hum - ble, There's no — place like home. A
moth - er now thinks — of her child. As she

GRANDFATHER'S CLOCK

HENRY C. WORK

Allegretto moderato

1. My grand-fa-ther's clock was too large for the shelf, So it stood nine-ty years on the
2. In watch - ing its pen - du - lum swing to and fro, Man-y hours had he spent while a

floor, ——— It was tall - er by half than the old man him-self, Though it
boy, ——— And in child - hood and man-hood the clock seem'd to know - And to

weighed not a pen - ny weight more. ——— It was bought on the morn of the
share both his grief and his joy. ——— For it struck twen-ty four when he

day that he was born, And was al - ways his treas - ure and pride.) — But it
en - ter'd at the door, With a bloom - ing and beau - ti - ful bride.

stopp'd   short,   Nev-er to go a-gain, When the old   man

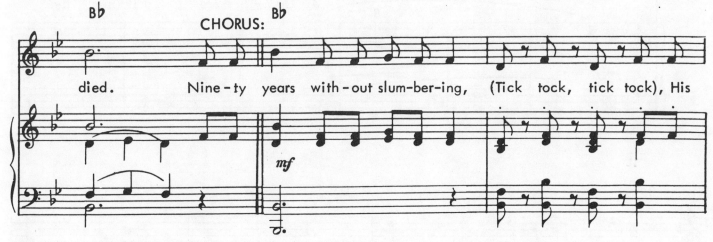

CHORUS:

died.   Nine-ty years with-out slum-ber-ing, (Tick tock, tick tock), His

life sec-onds num-ber-ing, (Tick tock, tick tock), It stopp'd   short,

Nev-er to go a-gain, When the old   man   died. ———

WHEN THE SAINTS GO MARCHING IN

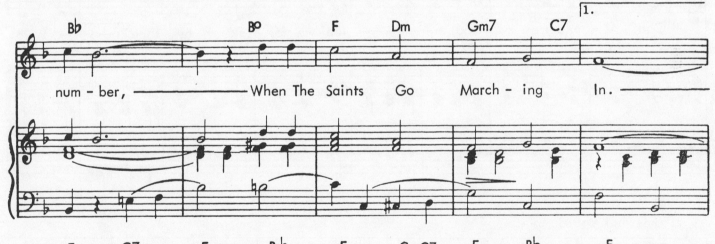

ELI ELI

Slowly, with reverence

Traditional Hebrew Chant

VOICE

God, Al - might - y God! ——— Are we for-sak-en by Thee? ———
E - li, E - li! ——— *lo - mo a - sav - to ni!* ———

God, Al - might - y God! ——— Are we for-sak-en by Thee? ——— With
E - li, E - li! ——— *lo - mo a - sav - to - ni!* ——— In

(Somewhat faster)

fire ——— and flame, Suf-f'ring pain and grief ———, E - ven put to shame, With no
Feu - er und Flamm hat man uns ge - brennt, ü - ber - all ge - macht uns zu

sign of Thy re-lief —, Yet no-one could suc-ceed - In turn-ing us from Thee —, From — Thee our
Schand'und zu Spott, doch ab-zu-wen-den hat uns kei-ner nich ge-kennt von — Dir, mein

God, —— From Thy Ho - ly To - rah — and Thy Ho-ly Law. God, oh God! Do
Gott, — von dein heil - ge Tot - re — und — dein Ge - bot. E - li, E - li!

not for-sake us, we — pray! God, oh God! Do not for - sake us, we pray!
lo-mo a-sav-to - ni! E - li, E - li! lo-mo a-sav-to - ni!

Night and day — How we pray — To - Thee - our — God! With fear we guard Thy
Tag und Nacht — nur ich tracht von Dir, — mein — Gott! Ich hüt mit Moi - re

HAVAH NAGILAH

Traditional Hebrew Song

Allegro marcato

Ha - vah _____ na - gi - lah, Ha - vah _____ na - gi - lah,
Ha - vah _____ na - gi - lah, Ha - vah _____ na - gi - lah,

Ha - vah _____ na - gi - lah, vay - nis - m' - chayh,
Ha - vah _____ na - gi - lah, Sing! Let us re - joice!

Ha - vah _____ na - gi - lah, Ha - vah _____ na - gi - lah,
Ha - vah _____ na - gi - lah, Ha - vah _____ na - gi - lah,

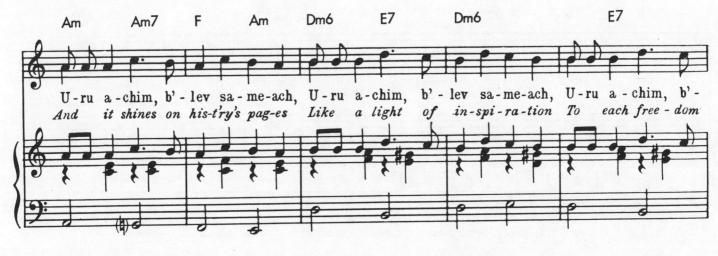

THE PALMS
(LES RAMEAUX)

Jean-Baptiste Faure

AULD LANG SYNE

Moderato

ROBERT BURNS

Should auld ac-quaint-ance be for-got, And nev-er brought to mind? Should

auld ac-quaint-ance be for-got, And days of auld lang syne?

REFRAIN

For auld lang syne, my dear, For auld lang syne, We'll

take a cup o' kind-ness yet, For auld lang syne.

SILENT NIGHT, HOLY NIGHT

Moderato

FRANZ GRUBER

Si - lent night, Ho — ly night, All is calm, All is bright,

'Round yon Vir — gin Moth-er and Child, Ho — ly In - fant so ten - der and mild,

Sleep in heav - en-ly peace ——, Sleep — in heav - en-ly peace.

German Text

1. *Stille Nacht! heilige Nacht!*
Alles schläft, einsam wacht,
Nur das traute, hoch heilige Paar
Holder Knabe mit locking Haar,
Schlaf' in himmlischer Ruh',
Schlaf' in himmlischer Ruh'.

2. *Stille Nacht! heilige Nacht!*
Hirten erst Kund gemacht
Durch der Engel Haleluja
Tönt es laut von fern und nah:
Christ, der Retter, ist da,
Christ, der Retter, ist da!

3. *Stille Nacht! heilige Nacht!*
Gottes Sohn, o wie lacht
Leib aus deinem göttlichen Mund,
Da uns schlägt die rettende Stund',
Christ, in deiner Geburt,
Christ, in deiner Geburt!

IT CAME UPON THE MIDNIGHT CLEAR

Words by
E. H. SEARS

Music by
R. S. WILLIS

O COME ALL YE FAITHFUL
(ADESTE FIDELES)

Translation by:
REV. JOHN READING

Latin Hymn

THE STAR SPANGLED BANNER

Words By
FRANCIS SCOTT KEY

Music by
JOHN S. SMITH

YOU'RE A GRAND OLD FLAG

GEORGE M. COHAN

You're a grand old flag, You're a high fly-ing flag, And for-ev-er, in peace, may you wave. You're the em-blem of the land I love, The home of the free and the

HAIL TO THE CHIEF

Words by
ALBERT GAMSE

Music by
JAMES SANDERSON

Tempo di marcia

Hail to the Chief we have chos-en for the na - tion,

Hail to the Chief! We sa - lute him, one and all.

Hail to the Chief, as we pledge co-op - er - a - tion

THE NAVY HYMN
(ETERNAL FATHER)

Text by
REV. WILLIAM WHITING

Music by
REV. JOHN B. DYKES

1. E - ter - nal Fa - ther, strong to save, Whose arm hath bound the rest-less wave, Who
2. E - ter - nal Fa - ther, lend Thy grace — To those with wings who fly thro' space, Thro'
3. Oh Tri - ni - ty of love and pow'r, Our breth-ren shield in dan-ger's hour, From

bidd'st the might-y o - cean deep, Its own ap - point - ed lim - its keep. Oh
wind and storm, thro' sun and rain, Oh bring them safe - ly home a - gain. Oh
rock and tem - pest, fire and foe, Pro - tect them where so e'er they go. Thus

hear us when we cry to Thee, For those in per - il on the sea! A - men.
Fa - ther, hear a hum-ble prayer, For those in per - il in the air! A - men.
ev - er - more shall rise to Thee - Glad hymns of praise from land and sea! A - men.